CW00382452

KNOWING THE TRUTH
First Series

Your Monthly Empowering
Words of Wisdom

Freedom from painful thoughts
How not to take things personal
How do you use grace for healing

LARGE PRINT

By Minister Alain Dagba

Divine Source Ministries
Brockton, MA
www.dsmchrist.org

- **Read**
- **Meditate**
- **Practice**
- **Grow in faith**
- **See Results**
- **It's that simple**

THIS MONTH SCRIPTURE

2 Corinthians 10:5

*"We demolish arguments and
every pretension that sets itself
up against the knowledge of God, and
we take captive every thought to make it
obedient to Christ."*

THE LESSON

To demolish is to make non-existent. God has given us the power to make the things that are not real lose existence, first in the mind, and then in our affairs.

You see, I want you to see a very important pattern here. I want you to see a result. Therefore, read the following truth again and try your best to see a pattern in it.

God has given us the power to make the things that are not real lose existence, first in the mind, and then in our affairs.

Now, I want you to make this truth your own. Close your eyes for a moment and take a deep breath. When you feel calm enough inside, repeat these words several times with conviction: *"God has given me the power to make things that are not real lose existence, first in my mind, and then in my affairs".*

You see, your inner transformation takes place only when your soul is convinced about the truth you hear.

The power of God moves through your conviction. This is important to know. What we call conviction is nothing else but your faith at its beginning stage. Conviction is faith as mustard seed. Everything begins with a conviction.

However, as you already know, you have to build this conviction. In order to build this conviction, you have to repeat the truth into your soul. This is a form of unceasing prayer. You have to pray the truth into your spirit.

First, you listen, and then you hear. Hearing is understanding. As you continue to pray the truth into your spirit, you will move from hearing to accepting. Acceptance is what will lead to faith. Faith is a change in consciousness.

Once this change takes places, your perception of outside conditions changes, and these conditions have no other choice but to change by allowing themselves to be affected by the truth that flows out through your thoughts, your words, your feelings, and actions.

Paul said, *"We demolish arguments".* Arguments are thoughts that have no source of truth. Sometimes we even have arguments with ourselves in our own mind. We do this by conducting thoughts that cannot build us spiritually.

Paul said that *"Brothers, whatever is true, whatever is noble, whatever is right, whatever is pure, whatever is lovely, whatever is admirable, if anything is excellent or praiseworthy, think about such things"* (Philippians 4: 8).

If you noticed, in everything above that was named by Paul, nothing was bad or negative. This is the proof that *positive thinking* is not created by man, but is an inspiration from God, known to his apostles.

I am about to tell you something you must be prepared for, because it is not in conformity with what the world made so many people believe, even in our churches.

This is it: *God thinks only good, for everything he has created is good.* I want you to read this again. *God thinks only good, for everything he has created is good.*

Now, this is leading us to the second idea, which is consequential to the first.

This is it: *Everything that is not good will bring mental arguments in the mind.*

Take sometimes to contemplate the above idea. And remember, things are not bad in themselves all the time. Things could be bad by your own perception of them. Therefore, we are talking about everything you define and perceive as bad.

Ponder on this one more time:

Everything that is not good will bring mental arguments in the mind.

Now, another idea is coming that you may not be familiar with, but this idea will help you understand what Jesus meant by *"there is no truth in the devil".*

Here it is: *Thoughts that are not good are not real, because only Truth could create reality, and God is Truth. Christ said, "I am the truth".*

What are we saying here? We are saying that that which is not created by God or Truth is not real. For everything God has created or Truth has created is good. Goodness is the mark of Truth. Now, do you believe this? This is the big question. I will say it again.

Only Truth creates reality. Thoughts that are not good are not real, because only Truth could create reality, and God is Truth. Christ said, "I am the truth".

We are saying that that which is not created by God or Truth is not real. For everything God has created or Truth has created is good. Goodness is the mark of Truth.

If there is a fight in you to accept this, do not worry or panic. This is because you have heard something before, which you have repeated so much to yourself, which is now fighting against God's wisdom.

You can now see the weakest point of your faith, and this is good. It is your false perception or definition of reality. This is the place you have the choice to gain the absolute power to demolish arguments (*opposing thoughts*), which stand against the knowledge of God.

Do you know God? This is the point my dear. If you know God as the source of nothing else but good, then you will withdraw power from the awareness of who you know he is to demolish any thought that has no essence of good.

Now, let us repeat what we have learned so far. Close your eyes to go deep within, calm your thoughts through deep breathing, and repeat with absolute conviction:

- *God has given me the power to make things that are not real lose existence, first in my mind, and then in my affairs.*

- *God thinks only good, for everything he has created is good.*

- *Everything that is not good will bring mental arguments in the mind.*

- *Thoughts that are not good are not real, because only Truth could create reality, and God is Truth. Christ said, "I am the truth".*

- *Only Truth creates reality. Thoughts that are not good are not real, because only Truth could create reality, and God is Truth. Christ said, "I am the truth".*

Jesus said, *"Only God is good."*

Luke 18: 19

If God is good and God is Truth, then Truth is good. If Truth is the only creator of Reality, and the effect of all things must resemble their cause, then Truth can only create good.

You see, knowing God as nothing else but good, and knowing the essence of Jesus as Christ, which is of the same nature as God, is Eternal Life.

Jesus defined Eternal Life this way: *"Now this is eternal life: that they know you, the only true God, and Jesus Christ, whom you have sent"* (John 17: 3).

Eternal Life is the full awakening of the Nature of God in us through the knowledge of God, which brings salvation in mind, body, and affairs.

Who is God to you? Do you see God as someone who could inflict pain in order to discipline you, like most people say, or do you see God as a father who cannot harm his own child?

You see, the way you see God is what will determine the kind of thoughts that will rule over your mind and your affairs. In the Old Testament, God was viewed as a principle, or the law of cause and effect, eye for eye, tooth for tooth, sowing and reaping. When you hurt them and they feel pain, they translate this as God telling them to hurt you back or war against you. And the people of the Old Testament, including the prophets, acted just like that principle they called "Lord", because they believe this is the way God is. Jesus, on the contrary, came to reveal the fatherhood of God to us, which is absolute good.

Because Jesus knew God, not in a shadow like the people of the Old Testament, but in the light, he was able to tell us that eye for eye; tooth for tooth is not the way to go. Instead, loving our enemies and do good to those who persecute us is the right way to go. For Jesus, this is the only way we could be called the children of our Father in heaven.

Jesus taught us to see things from their essence, from reality, from their cause, which is in God or Truth. For example, the person you call your *enemy* is in real essence the image and the likeness of God. The problem is, because your mind is infected with a false perception of reality, the personality of the enemy is all that you can see.

Jesus knew that as we know only good to be the real essence of things, we could love the image and the likeness of God in the so-called "enemies", pray for them from this awareness, and allow the power of God to flow through us and save them from the false personality called "enemy".

This false personality has no ground in Truth. It is been created by life painful experiences. The statement that the things we go through in life become personalities in us is true.

These negative personalities the Bible calls them *"the children of the devil"*. This is because they have never been created by God, but by our own mind based on the way we interpret our life experiences. For example, a father who has been abused ends up abusing his children. People hurt each other with their wounds. With this understanding, there is no need to take anything personal.

Now, what are you going to do about this? This is the question. We may say, as we often do, that it is the devil acting. Yes, but do not forget that the devil is also personalities acting through you and others.

People have their personal painful stories, and you have your own. Therefore, you must always be tolerant toward yourself and others. This will bring you true healing and the power to bestow forgiveness upon others. Once you are able to do this, you can call on God's grace at all times to help you love yourself in others, and save both you and them from the reactions of all false personalities.

We have internal demons. Anger, impatience, resentment, lust, and all the negative things that we emotionally or physically manifest, they are indeed nothing else but personalities or demons in us. God did not create these personalities. The totality of these personalities is what we call the sinful nature. They are not who we are in essence. These personalities in charge of creating arguments and pretensions in mind, we must be set free from.

You are not these personalities or this sinful nature in essence. What is reality cannot be altered. What is created by Truth cannot be changed. If you were in essence these personalities, then there cannot be salvation. They must remain forever. However, we know this is not the case. You are the image and the likeness of God in essence. This "YOU" had been created by Truth. Do you accept this?

Paul, personifying this sinful nature as "sin" said: *"And if I do what I do not want to do, I agree that the law is good. As it is, it is no longer I myself who do it, but it is sin living in me. For I know that good itself does not dwell in me, that is, in my sinful nature. For I have the desire to do what is good, but I cannot carry it out. For I do not do the good I want to do, but the evil I do not want to do--this I keep on doing. Now if I do what I do not want to do, it is no longer I who do it, but it is sin living in me that does it. For in my inner being I delight in God's law; but I see another law at work in me, waging war against the law of my mind and making me a prisoner of the law of sin at work within me."*

(Romains 7: 16-23)

Who hurts others through you? It is not the image and the likeness of God that you are in essence. Who speaks through you? Who feels through you? Who sees through you? Who acts through you?

It is time, I believe, to face these real questions, and you know what I am talking about. Christianity is not a fairytale. It is a real life transforming ground.

The "sin" or the personalities of pain, lust, hurt, envy, jealousy, greed, anger, etc., which are living through us will not stand if we make a decision to claim who we really are in essence.

The one we call Satan or the devil was not a direct creation of God. God created a beautiful angel called Lucifer, which means "The Bringer of Light", because God creates only good.

However, this angel also corrupted himself with another personality through his own corrupted desires and false interpretation of the reality of God, just like us, and his sinful personality is what we call "Satan". It has no essence of Truth, because was never created by God or by "Good".

Blaming Satan all the time for our shortcomings should not make us look on the outside all the time, but also look on the inside. What are your inner devils? What are the pains and false knowledge you have not dealt with or you have left sitting in your souls, or that you are afraid to confront?

The one called the adversary cannot create Reality. He is a master of illusions, which you make real with your own belief.

For example, if the devil in you makes your mother look like a witch, will you believe it, or go beyond and see the image and the likeness of God in your mother, and pray for her from that perspective thus see the power of God move to set your mind free and your mother free?

I told you before that Christianity is a practical knowledge. I believe by now you realize it for yourself.

These negative personalities who do evil things through us are from their father, the inner devil living in us or the sinful nature. They are not what we are in essence. Jesus was able to recognize them when they talked through the Pharisees. He told the Pharisees the following words:

"You belong to your father, the devil, and you want to carry out your father's desires. He was a murderer from the beginning, not holding to the truth, for there is no truth in him. When he lies, he speaks his native language, for he is a liar and the father of lies"

(John 8: 44)

Desires come from within. They could be either from your true essence, which is the image and the likeness of God or Good, or from the personality of sin.

Jesus said that in the devil there is no truth but only lies. He said that lying is his native language, which means he was born from a place that has no substance of truth.

We know that only Truth can create reality. Truth is God. The Truth is what is in the mind of God and is eternal in nature. Please repeat this for a few times:

Truth is God. The Truth is what is in the mind of God and is eternal and good in nature.

Consequently, the devil cannot create reality but illusions. This is why your sickness cannot be eternal. This is why your problems cannot be eternal. They have no other ground of real existence besides your own mind, using your belief in them for root to persist.

Reality is born out of truth, but illusion is born out of lies. If you believe in illusions, you will create arguments in your mind. Arguments bring confusion. Confusion brings doubt. Doubt brings fear. Fear brings destruction.

The Bible says that we are not given the spirit of fear. So we must not come to allow fear in our mind. The one who is victim of fear has been captured by strong illusions in the mind.

Paul says that we have the power to demolish all forms of arguments and pretentions. My question is do you believe this?

This power is the ability you have to hold the single truth in mind that only God is Truth, only Truth creates Reality, and only Reality is good.

Anything that is not good or does not make us feel good whether in appearance or in heart, must not be believed as being from God. Eternal

Life is to know God. Jesus said only God is good.

Pretentions here are things that sound and look as fact and appear very bold, but are not real in essence. Arguments and pretentions set themselves up against the knowledge of God and Christ.

If your mind is clouded by un-realness, you cannot see the good that God is and has for you. You cannot see the good in yourself. You cannot see the good in others. Therefore, you will unceasingly sow thoughts and feelings of opposite of good and reap them as sickness in your body and misfortunes in your affairs.

We must know that God is good in essence. Yet, if we let our mind be filled with illusions, we will lose the truth that God in his nature is only good.

Consequently, we come to believe in a tyrannical and unkind God, which the personality of sin wants us to see.

Your belief in the realness of evil is the root of the evil you experience. This is the greatest sin the human race must be set free from.

Many times in the scripture, Jesus compared man to a *tree*, his beliefs to a *root*, and his actions, choices, and life to *fruits*. It is for a reason. He said, *"Every plant that my heavenly*

Father has not planted will be pulled up by the roots" (Matthew 15: 13)

The belief that evil is created by God or evil is from the essence of Truth must die in the name of Jesus. Once it dies within, it withers on the outside, for our outer conditions have their root in our souls, which he called the storehouse.

Jesus said, *"Make a tree good and its fruit will be good, or make a tree bad and its fruit will be bad, for a tree is recognized by its fruit. You brood of vipers, how can you who are evil say anything good? For the mouth speaks what the heart is full of. A good man brings good things out of the good stored up in him, and an evil man brings evil things out of the evil stored up in him. But I tell you that everyone will have to give account on the day of judgment for every empty word they have spoken."* (Matthew 12: 35).

Jesus also said, *"By their fruit you will recognize them. Do people pick grapes from thornbushes, or figs from thistles? Likewise, every good tree bears good fruit, but a bad tree bears bad fruit. A good tree cannot bear bad fruit, and a bad tree cannot bear good fruit"* (Matthew 7: 16-18).

It is either we believe the Christ we claim to follow or we fall. It is this simple. Moreover, if we want to follow him, we must begin to make practical his teachings. The Bible says that the son of God or the Christ is the image of God, the exact representation of his being. And, we are also created in the same image and likeness. No wonder Paul boldly declared that "he" as human nature, no longer lives, but Christ, as divine nature now lives in him. Could we do the same thing?

The Bible says to *"count yourself dead to sin, but alive to God in Christ Jesus" (Romans 6: 11).* This means you have to be the one to consciously do this.

We have the power to take captive every thought and to make it obedient to Christ. Our true nature as new creations in Christ is identical to Christ. Through faith, we have become the *"Christs"* of God, and this is why Paul said we have the mind of Christ.

You cannot have someone's mind and not be like him, for as a man thinks so is he. The mind of Christ does not create negative and evil thoughts arguing against the will of Christ.

It is only when you claim your divine new nature in consciousness that you have the power to take these arguing thoughts into captivity and you make them obedient to Christ. There is no other way.

We make these arguments and pretensions obedient to our new

nature in Christ by faith. Because these thoughts run endlessly in the mind, we must first take them captive before we could make them slave to the Christ within.

Now, I have a practice for you. Get in the habit of practicing examining your thoughts. If the thought is not good, then it is from the adversary, not from God.

If the thought is not good, then it is not real. It is an illusion because it has no essence and no place in God's mind. It has no permanency.

If it has no place in God's mind then it must have no place in the mind of Christ, which is your mind as a new creation in God.

Once the thought appears, tell the thought: *"I see no illusion in the mind of Christ, so all arguments and pretentions are now called null and void in the name of Jesus Christ".*

Practice your faith

What have you learned through the reading of this booklet/ Write everything down with no exception. You do not have to write everything down today. Take your time

....

....

....

....

....

....

....

....

....

....
....

....
....
....
....
....
....
....
....
....
....
....

....
....
....
....
....
....
....
....

....
....
....

....
....
....
....
....
....
....
....
....
....
....

Write down some points that were challenging to you in this booklet. Be honest with yourself.

....
....
....
....

....
....
....
....
....
....
....

....
....
....
....
....
....
....
....
....
....
....

....
....
....

....
....
....
....
....
....
....
....

**Have you fully accepted these challenging
points? Explain your answer.**

....
....
....
....
....
....
....
....
....
....
....

Write down everything this book has called you to change about yourself and your life.

....

....

....

....

....

....

....

....

....

....

....

....

....

....

....

....

....

....

....
....
....

What is your definition of reality?

....
....
....
....
....
....
....
....
....
....
....

What will you then say was the power of Jesus to love unconditionally?

....
....
....

....

....

....

....

....

....

....

....

Write yourself a letter concerning the way you ought to perceive life from this point on.

(Your first name),

....

....

....

....

....

....

....

....

....

....
....

....
....
....
....
....
....
....
....
....
....
....

....
....
....
....
....
....
....
....

....
....
....

How will you say this book was able to help your faith in Christ?

....
....
....
....
....
....
....
....
....
....
....

....
....
....
....

....
....
....
....
....

....
....
....
....
....
....
....

Visit www.dsmchrist.org to leave your
testimony to inspire others

THANK YOU

Printed in Great Britain
by Amazon

22983635R00030